10 Steps to Healing a Broken Heart

10 Steps to Healing a Broken Heart

By Judine T. Hitchmon

10 Steps to Healing a Broken Heart

Copyright © 2018 by Judine T. Hitchmon

ISBN 978-1-7326161-1-0

*This book is in dedication to all those whose heart have a beat,
missed a beat, or need a beat.*

10 Steps to Healing a Broken Heart

Contents

If you love them, then love in the way that frees them. Build them up. Grow them and let them grow you. Love that is confining, restrictive and full of laws is love born out of the desperation of loneliness. - JM Storm

Introduction

As complicated as I know love can be, I don't think I could wish it were simple. For as many times as I have had my heart broken, I still find joy in new love and romance as if I had never had my heart broken. It's wild, I know. What can I say? I'm a free spirit, and I am free-spirited in love. Unfortunately, that never dulls the pain, and so, from time to time, my heart is broken, and it's time to do the work.

What work you ask? Well, relationship work. Heartbreaks are unfortunately a part of the experience of relationships. Heartbreak isn't necessarily one event, but a series of events that make it difficult for us to move on in the most appropriate direction, leading to scarring and unresolved grief. People are not perfect. They will disappoint you, hurt you, and sometimes make you angry (and these are not even the least of the emotions you can experience when sharing your time and energy with another). Sometimes these trespasses can deepen a relationship, stagnate the relationship, or even end the relationship entirely. Either path is a struggle and will require strength, commitment, and trust, whether that is in oneself or in the perception of the pair.

This is WHERE things get complicated. Who is it going to be—you or the pair? The answer to this question will be the determinant on your next course of actions. Many times this is the question we all fail to answer, and we have heartbreak that leaves scars and unresolved grief. The moment we feel we are compromising who we are, for the worse to maintain the pair, is the moment we need to choose self. And that's a hard decision to make because that means you become aware that the person you love

1

and care for is not only damaging the pair, but damaging themselves. This is WHAT makes things complicated.

When we love and care for someone, we want the best for them, even if they don't see it for themselves. It's human nature. Logically though, we can't make anyone see anything unless they too perceive it for themselves. This means if what you see for someone is based on love and care, if they love and care for themselves too, it won't be long before they see what you see and then you compromise. If the pair isn't on the same page, there can be no negotiation. With no negotiation, there is no compromise. With no compromise, a relationship will lead to an end and this is HOW things get complicated.

Some things must come to an end. How complicated is that? Well, when you're not ready, it's very complicated. So how do you prepare yourself for an untimely end? It's not going to be simple, but in the end, it will be helpful (Trust me, I've been there several times.). And honestly, it's not even about an end of a pair. It's about the beginning of choosing you when it's necessary for you. When we enter into relationships, we blend energies with one another. At the time when things end, we need a process on how to get back to the energy of self. The concepts laid out in this book are structured for just that—getting back to self.

Some of us think holding on makes us strong, but sometimes it is letting go.- Herman Hesse

Step 1

Let Go!

I know what you're thinking. This is probably the last thing you would want to do, but I promise it's not what you think. When I say let go, I mean validate your emotions. Take time to recognize, acknowledge, and quell all the feelings associated with the pangs of loss. And it is the first step because the beginning is when it hurts the most. The beginning is where the mismanagement of our emotions can create consequences we can otherwise avoid; consequences that keep us dwelling in our pain, causing sufferance ... so, let go!

As the old adage says, "Time heals all wounds," and it does, partly. Time allows for you to think objectively about a situation. Time tells you to move forward because it moves forward. Time tells you to go on no matter what because it does. But time does nothing for you because time only knows one thing: Move forward no matter what.

Make time work for you. Understand that while you may not have total control over time, you do have control over what you do with the time you have. Tell yourself how much time you will devote to letting go. Make a plan and stick to it. Outlining how you will respond to your environment lends you power and control - much of what we feel is taken from us when we suffer a loss.

Is it easy? Hell no! It's hard to take a look at what makes us hurt, call it a name, and let it still dwell inside of us. That's the thing about emotions. You can't cherry pick them. If you have one, you can have them all. The key to managing your emotions is to endure positive ones and only tolerate negative ones. At least you are the one that gets to decide how you let go either way, and since time is definitely moving forward, you might as well move side by side.

How do you do this, you ask? Through the process of "feeling identification". Recognition of your emotions is part of the process of feeling identification. Taking control of your time to heal requires action. You have to "get" where you are emotionally, determine if you have been here before (if you haven't, choose where you want to go with it), and devise a plan to let go.

"Getting" where you are emotionally is developing an understanding of what brought you to your current emotional state. You are probably thinking, What if I don't know how I'm feeling? or What if I can't explain how I feel? When we don't know something we need to know, we find out. That is action. Ask yourself questions and answer them. For example, what breaks your heart? Is it the idea that someone doesn't want you anymore? Do you feel rejected? Does that make you want to cry? Asking questions based on what you already know about yourself increases your self-awareness, and self-awareness includes the ability to identify and quell your emotions. Oh, and please don't ever ask why. "Why" leads to defensiveness and defensiveness is self-justifying and distrustful ... let go.

If you have been here before, what did you do to move past the hurt? Did it work? I mean, if you are here again, maybe it did or maybe it will again. But don't forget to think about where you were in space and time. Things could have been different. You were different. This time it's different—with your head thrown back, tongue out, crying. Take what you can and let go.

If you haven't had the pleasure of your heart being ripped out before, then this is the opportune time to create a space for acceptance of the broken you. And this is important because you need an experience to "survive" from. This is the moment where you can identify barriers to your happiness, and more importantly, how you can be loved even with your flaws, because if you can love yourself, flaws and all, someone else can too. This is the moment where you "get" that nothing is perfect and sometimes things do fall apart. That's a notch on the belt ... let it go.

Poor planning leads to poor performance. I know you've heard this before, but it's not rhetoric. If you plan to do nothing, nothing gets done and you will quickly lose sight of your power to let go. You are the one in control, which makes you the "[wo]man with the plan." Put a cut on it and give yourself a time-frame. Commit to tasks that keep you enduring positive emotions because activity affects mood. Elicit support when you need it most. And more importantly, just do it and let go

Let's Practice!

Part of increasing your self-awareness involves having the ability to recognize emotions you experience both in depth and intensity. The depth of the emotion would be the emotion in its broadest sense, and the intensity of the emotion would be specific to the depth. Complete this chart to identify the depth the intensity of your emotions, and build your feelings vocabulary to understand where you are emotionally.

Ex: Happy is broad. Specific emotions you can experience in happiness are calm, peace, neutral, etc.

Depth (broad)	Intensity (specific)
Happiness	joyful _____ _____ _____ _____ _____ _____ _____ _____ _____ _____ _____ _____ _____ _____ _____ _____
Sadness	grief _____ _____ _____ _____ _____ _____ _____ _____ _____ _____ _____ _____ _____ _____ _____ _____
Anger	upset _____ _____ _____ _____ _____ _____ _____ _____ _____ _____ _____ _____ _____ _____ _____ _____
Fear	scared _____ _____ _____ _____ _____ _____ _____ _____ _____ _____ _____ _____ _____ _____ _____ _____

In order to know ourselves better we must ask the right questions.

Of the emotions you listed – what emotion do you feel you struggle with the most? Is it a broad emotion or specific?
What specific situations bring about this emotion?
What feelings can you experience to replace specific negative emotions?
What can you do to bring about the emotions you desire?

Pretty words are not always true, and true words are not always pretty. -Unknown

Step 2

Believe It!

"How could this happen to me?!"

I can hear you now screaming at the top of your lungs, desperate for an answer. The truth is, when we look to other people to give us an answer, we oftentimes become disillusioned by their perspective. In the end, people will always be willing to tell you what you did wrong, and how you are the one to blame. While it may be hurtful, believe it.

I know, I know. The last thing you want to do is blame yourself, too, but belief is about acceptance. Think about it. In the end, people tend to feel free to tell you all the faults they see in you without reservation. It is in that moment where sometimes you don't even have to ask, that moment your self-esteem is shattered into pieces of what you let them construct. That's okay, though. Self-awareness is about knowing what crumbles your glass house down to the ground. Believe it.

This is what makes it so important for us to accept what others see as flaws in our being. When you accept another's perspective of you, it returns power back to you. In this way, you can decide whether you want to change or not. It also provides you an opportunity to develop insight into who you are, making each brutal fact purposeful in the development of your being. The more you know about self, the more you know about others. Believe it.

Sometimes it may seem easier to believe that a person has had their soul abducted by aliens, and the version you now know is unfamiliar with the way of the world. But ask yourself, can you love an alien? You have to accept that sometimes you may want something, but when things happen outside of your favor, you have to change your mind. The last place you want to end up is in the Twilight Zone. Believe it.

You have to know that anxiety is very necessary but can be a self-sabotaging emotion when unmanaged. Anxiety, when triggered, can send you on a hyper-vigilant journey of survival just for breathing sake. Anxiety, by definition, is real or perceived fear of the unknown and can trigger a biological response of fight, flight, or freeze as a result of your breathing patterns. If you are asking yourself, who is this stranger? Then whomever they have become is unfamiliar to you. Are you going to let an alien take you to outer space? Because, you can't breathe out there. Believe it.

As much as you would like to wish this was a bad dream you will soon wake up from, it isn't. When the masks are finally off and you get to see someone for who they truly are, you can sometimes get stuck in disbelief, idle as if people can never be someone other than what they put off. When in hindsight, you can connect all the dots, which usually point to all of what you are now aware of. Point is, when you see it, believe it.

Let's Practice!

Practicing self-awareness requires an understanding that you are not perfect, but will remain true to self throughout the process of change. We all have faults, but only those aware of their faults can change them (or make certain they do not become our detriments).

	Name 3 things you could improve on regarding communication:
	1.
	2.
	3.
	Name 3 things you could improve on regarding personal boundaries:
	1.
	2.
	3.
	Name 3 things you could improve on regarding self-care:
	1.
	2.
	3.
	Name 3 things you could improve on regarding self-esteem:
	1.
	2.
	3.

Everything we see is a shadow cast by that which we do not see. - Martin Luther King Jr.
Step 3

In the Shadow

When all else seems to fail and you have lived day one and/or two for the last few weeks like Ground Hog Day, know that there is a shadow. All of us have one--a place where our deepest sorrows and humiliations go when the endurance of an experience has turned into a fear that you may be transformed for the worse, and you must act quickly to preserve self.

Hide your experience in the shadow. I mean "hide" with great discretion. More specifically, I mean hide as in containment. If this experience has left you out of control, then regain control through the acceptance of darkness. Most people need this dark space, this dungeon in our mind that makes everything negative disappear from sight. By not giving your current reality light, it creates a perspective of least resistance. Least resistance creates avenues for forward motion. Move with time, not against it. Put it in the shadow.

You must know, though, in darkness all things are distorted. I mean, that is the whole purpose of putting it in the dark. If it is obscure to us in reality, then darkness lends to its insignificance. Darkness has no shape, no life, no light. The tricky part is all things that are decided to go into the shadow are there because of their significance. Unpack when you have the heart, but until then put it in the shadow.

Now, just because you don't put light on something, doesn't mean it doesn't exist. That's another thing you must always remember when putting something in the shadow. Oh, and don't think this is the first thing going in the shadow. You have been putting things in the shadow since you were born, which means the shadow is in everyone. If you feel this heartache has left you in the dark, maybe they have put you in the shadow. So, where do they go? In the shadow.

Create an alter ego. When putting things in the dark, we have to replace an old perspective with a new one that will constitute a stronger sense of self. If you could have planned this, how would you have liked to experience it? (Remember, you need to be comfortable with having to put things in the shadow, so negative experiences are also opportunities for growth. What do you need to come out of the dark thinking, feeling, and doing? After all, everyone can't know what you have in the dark or it wouldn't be your dark space. And know that all is not lost. Put the situation in the shadow, but leave the dark with the light that is still in you.

Let's Practice!

The ability to distract your thoughts and actions yet remain focused on the purpose of that distraction is a skill, and must be practiced. This allows for the use of the defense mechanism compartmentalization, and ultimately rationalization. If you feel like life is over because your relationship is, then you must remind yourself that your life and your relationship are two separate entities, distract!

Healthy Distractions	
Identify different types of distractions for each category.	

Physical ex: go to gym	Mental ex: complete a puzzle
1.	1.
2.	2.
3.	3.
4.	4.
5.	5.

Emotional ex: listen to inspirational song	Spiritual ex: attend yoga class
1.	1.
2.	2.
3.	3.
4.	4.
5.	5.

If you don't like something change it. If you can't change it, change your
attitude. -Maya Angelou

Step 4

Learn to Make Adjustments

Change is hard for everyone and even harder for those who don't know how to affect change, particularly the change which is required when things don't go as planned and when what was planned involves another person. What if I were to tell you there is a process for change, too? There are identifiable stages you will move through using components of your self-awareness. This process is tried and true, but you must understand one crucial element: the only thing you can change is you. You have total control over your perspective and behavior, however, in order to lever your power over change, you need to have a good grasp of each of these concepts.

Self-awareness. Many people interchange this term with self-reflection or self-evaluation. They all take account of self but are significantly different. Self-awareness refers to a process which is constant, whereas reflection and evaluation refer to processes that have means to an end. In other words, awareness is about the past, the present, and the future. Self-awareness then affords you foresight, insight, and hindsight, all key components to affecting change. It is what tells you who you were, who you are, and who you are going to be without bias, for the condition of change. Adjust.

Radical Acceptance. The reality of the situation is you cannot change anyone. This means you cannot control what they think, feel, or do. You can affect it, but ultimately it is in their control which is radical acceptance. A lot of times our emotions trick us into believing our sufferance can be ended by avoidance of what is real. Avoidance is stagnation and adjustment is about action. The ability to accept the things you cannot change, only to focus on what you can change, always puts you in the position to make adjustments. Adjust.

Perspective. Last but not least, perspective is a major component to making adjustments. As I mentioned before, change is hard. When your heart is set on something or someone for whatever reason, any deviation from that which you hope for can taint your perception. You become disenfranchised from the rest of the world because now you are alone, at least that's the perception. And that's just it, perception is fluid, open for interpretation. Thankfully, you choose the interpretation. Ask yourself: What can I change here? What perspective do I need to make this adjustment? And adjust.

Let's Practice!

While fairytales may not always come true, you can have a piece of the magic. All you need is a magic wand! Learning to make adjustments needs imagination. Wave your wand to make things work for the best, but remember – the only person you have control over is you.

	What do I have the power to change in this situation?
	What do I need to think, and believe, in order to make this change?
	What evidence do I have that proves I am capable of change?

The secret of change is to focus all of your energy not on fighting the old, but on building the new. - Socrates

Step 5

Make Change

Now that you've accepted the fact that you can't control anyone but yourself and keeping your perceptions open for careful interpretation, it's time to get to work on the concept of change. Theoretically, there are several stages to the process of change. Utilizing this theory allows for a person to affect change in their behavior (Please note: thinking is a behavior). With that, just knowing how change occurs gives you the power to control it.

One of the most self-destructive behaviors you can engage in as an adult is living in blissful ignorance, yet blissful ignorance is the first step in the process of change. Ignorance, by itself, is understandable as we all have certain limitations on how we acquire knowledge as result of biology and/or experience. Just being ignorant to a subject only speaks to a lack of experience or awareness thus far, and not the inability to gain experience and perspective. Blissful ignorance is willful, purposed to ignore opportunities for growth until the seed is planted. The ability to make change means you plant your own seeds, and you do that by asking yourself the right questions to remain out of blissful ignorance.

When you ask yourself the right questions, you gain insight. That is an understanding of self that allows you to do one very important task—affect change. Insight is the second stage in the process of change. Insight introduces you to yourself. This is where you will discover things that you like, that you have to replace or modify because they are not working for you and you need that, particularly in a time when you are feeling the pain of your loss and trying to hold on to anything you can. You have to have a skill set that lets you like something but still let it go, for the sake of you. It is the "what" to the reason people change—self-preservation. Insight is about survival.

Life is essentially about survival of the fittest. We can interpret this in many ways, but without going too far down the rabbit hole, you have to be ready to survive! Readiness is the third stage in the process of change. The struggle of life is mostly measured by the preparedness of that individual. How prepared are you to see something that is hurting you and begin working immediately to preserve self? What actions will you take? What do you need to know? Who do you need to help? What's the plan? Get ready for action and survive to the fittest.

You have to be swift. Striking while the iron is hot is the best way to gain and keep momentum, and you are going to need motivation because nothing is perfect and sometimes things do fall apart, remember? That is neither here nor there, though. You are moving forward, and you can be confident that what is for you will be for you. And if it isn't, if nothing else, you can change your mind. This perspective can put you at ease for now, and whenever it doesn't, change.

Let's Practice!

What is familiar to you, will always be comfortable; and sometimes what comforts you, can also cripple you. How can you make yourself comfortable, even when you have been made to be uncomfortable? You get used to the unfamiliar.

	Try 3 new things you have never done before...
	ex: food of a different culture
	Process the experience
	1. **What feelings did you experience?**
	2. **How did you feel afterward?**
	3. **Would you do it again?**
	Learn 3 new things you are interested in...
	ex: learn a yo-yo trick
	Process the experience
	1. **Was it what you expected?**
	2. **What feelings surfaced?**
	3. **How can you use this new skill?**
	Go to 3 new places you have never been...
	ex: new museum or exhibit
	Process the experience
	1. **What did you learn?**
	2. **Were you able to use past knowledge of experience?**
	3. **What would make you share the experience?**

Emotions make us human. Denying them makes us beasts. –
Victoria Klein

Step 6

Keep Your Emotions in Check

I cannot be dismissive to the fact that heartbreak hurts! It's a real
thing. Emotions are real, but they are not tangible. What I mean
is, they become real when you make them real through
behavioral expression. Have you ever felt sad and not cried?
What is your perspective when you do cry?

 "OMG, this hurts!?"

That's the point. Keeping the experience of negative emotions
brief keeps you from enduring, and those thoughts are your
perspective. You can have a slew of emotions and act on them in
ways that are beneficial to self as opposed to a detriment to self.
Your perspective will dictate your emotions, and your emotions
will dictate your behavior (You know, Cognitive Behavioral
Therapy.). Keep your emotions in check.

Keeping your emotions in check is about survivorship. When it
comes to survival, your mentality can either be that of a victim or
a survivor. These two perspectives would render two opposite
outlooks, yet one thing ties them together—the experience. In
order for someone to become a survivor, at one point they were
the victim. This correlation illustrates how perspective can
change the expression of our emotion. You keep your emotions
in check with perspective. So, keep your emotions in check.

Acknowledgement is also crucial to keeping emotions in check.
Sometimes just being honest about how you are feeling to
yourself and others is good enough to quell your emotions. It's
called venting, but venting does nothing for your perspective and
it shouldn't. Well, not entirely. Venting is about validation. The
need for validation keeps us in a victim mentality and this is bad

for perspective. Not to say that a victim doesn't need validation. They do, but to a certain extent. You decide to which extent. Keep your emotions in check.

Survivors validate themselves. They don't wait around for people to understand where they are coming from or to tell them "sorry." They understand that those are not things self can control. They know they are responsible only for their own perspective and experience, and a survivorship mentality brings on feelings of empowerment and resilience. Think: What thoughts would a survivor have? What do you think they would tell themselves to move forward? Probably, "Keep your emotions in check."

Let's Practice!

One of the best ways to keep surviving to the fittest, is to remember what you have already survived. It keeps you motivated, and helps you to remember, that while you have had some tough moments, you also have had triumphs.

Survival Guide
What I have survived…
How I have survived…
What I will survive…
How I will survive…

In order to carry out a positive action we must develop a positive vision. –Dalai Lama

Step 7

Clean House

The new year cannot be the only time you organize your thoughts and set goals based on the perspective of a new and improved you. It needs to happen constantly! Every time you feel low or hurt, pick yourself up (and everything else around you for that matter), and create something new. How many times have you cleaned up and felt feelings of accomplishment? Cleaning house refers to more than just what is indicated. Something as simple as cleaning up and organizing your space leaves you with positive feelings. This is how we exchange emotions. Clean House.

Every second you experience negative emotions, you not only open yourself to self-destructive behaviors, but biological responses that can also keep you enduring negativity. Crying changes your breathing patterns as does anger and anxiety. Emotions hurt physically because of how our behavior affects us biologically, which is the response. Stress kills. Clean House.

Now, anxiety is the real kicker! Anxiety can be defined as a fear of real or perceived danger. Notice how the words real and perceived are used to differentiate in the definition. Real danger would be described as actual, while perceived danger—well, that's just a thought. When we experience heartache, it often feels scary because we don't know what to expect, but it's not life or death. When you are in actual danger, a life or death situation, your brain will go into a state of vigilance that allows for you to attempt survival. After a breakup, YOU remain, so you have survived. Clean house.

To your brain, survival is simply breathing normally. When we experience anxiety to the extent that we trigger the fight, flight, or freeze response, our brain will signal all logical functions to shut down until you resume your normal breathing cadence. It releases this chemical called cortisol which makes it impossible for the logical parts of your brain to communicate, all for the sake of breathing. Heartache is not life or death, even though we can agree it hurts. Your body is a temple after all. It will protect you from anything you would hold your breath on. Clean House.

Anxiety is essentially the fear of the unknown. When you don't know something, you find out. That is how you deal with anxiety. It's what makes us feel we always need clarity during a breakup. Oh, and then closure. The fact is, because we can't control what other people think, feel, or do, clarity and closure, as defined by the other, will never be enough. You have to quell your anxiety with what works for you. Do whatever you have to do to help yourself to stay clean in a dirty situation. Clean House.

Think of yourself as gold. You can be feather-light like the golden dust sprinkled in the universe, or you can be heavy as a ton of bricks. Enduring the feelings of heartache will leave you carrying your weight in gold. You can create your reality beginning with your thoughts, dress it up with your imagination, and manifest it into whatever you desire. If what you desire alerts danger, you will manifest heartache. Clean house.

Let's Practice!

Just breathe. Before you regain total control over self, you have to breathe -and there is a way do it. Relaxation breathing is essential to bringing adequate amounts of oxygen to your brain, and if this situation has you in a panic, you are definitely going to need to know exactly how to breathe to calm yourself down. Try it!

Relaxation Breathing Technique
Remember to breath in through your nose, and out through your mouth
STEP 1 - INHALE
take a deep breath in through your nose, for count of four seconds
STEP 2 - EXHALE
Breathe out slowly for a count of eight seconds
STEP 3 - REPEAT
Complete these step 1&2 for five cycles

Daring to set boundaries is about having the courage to love ourselves even when we risk disappointing others. -Brene Brown

Step 8

Build a Fence

Now that you have made yourself aware that there is a time and place for everything that is personal to you, it's time to establish boundaries. Creating personal boundaries is a powerful practice of happy people. Boundaries are set for two main reasons: for you to know how far to let people in, and for people to know how close they can come. We set these, sometimes invisible, markers as a protection of our being, physically, mentally, and emotionally. And the better you are at establishing boundaries, the less heartache you will experience in relationships. So, build a fence.

Physical boundaries are more than just the protection of your body. Your body is the first thing you need to build a fence around, that's the easy part. It is easy to identify ways in which we like to be physically touched and ways we do not like to be physically touched. It is what extends from our body that becomes difficult to protect because it is not so explicit like personal space and privacy. Both personal space and privacy are subjective, and because of that, conflict can arise in relationships. You must stand firm, though. Soft boundaries can become an invitation for people to violate you and make it tangible. Build a fence.

Mental boundaries include your ideas, thoughts, and beliefs, but mental boundaries are subjective as well and with good reason. You are an individual with individual needs based on your own culture, experience, knowledge, and so on. How you think is imperative to your behavior. Allowing others to permeate our thought process to the extent of destroying our esteem, advances their control over us, consequently rendering us powerless. Being a puppet leaves you with strings attached. Build a fence.

Emotional boundaries, again subjective, are by far the most difficult boundaries to establish than any other. You and everyone else have all rights to any emotion. After all, feelings are universal in that we all have established a consensus that they are real (Like I really needed to tell you that, right?). It is the perspective or behavior that led you to those emotions that need to be legitimatized. If you don't want to feel the way you do, you can exchange emotions. If you don't want others to make you feel the way you do, build a fence.

How do you set boundaries? In many ways. One key factor to establishing boundaries is by a mental health term referred to as "feeling identification." Your emotional responses are the key indicators to where opportunity for a boundary to be set is distinguished. Your negative responses give you clues to a boundary being overstepped. And while you may not want to establish that boundary within the emotion, reflection on the experience will surely give you resolve for future reference. Setting personal boundaries is a learned behavior, and it needs to be practiced. But waiting around like a sitting duck is target practice. Build a fence.

Let's Practice!

Establishing boundaries is an important self-care routine. Listed are 3 different types of boundaries. Identify boundaries you have already established for each category, and new boundaries you want to establish for self-care.

Physical Boundaries: (ex: touch, space, property, how people touch you)	
Emotional Boundaries: (ex: feelings, how people make you feel)	
Mental Boundaries: (ex: thoughts, how people make you think)	

Today you are you, that is truer than true. There is no one alive who is youer that you. – Dr. Seuss

Step 9

Re-introduce Yourself

How many times have you thought to yourself, If they could only see me now! It is what we think when we have recognized our growth and are proud of the results. This is not to declare the path of this journey was clear or without pain, or that you will only have to do it once in a lifetime. The statement simply states, "I have arrived. Look at me now." It's almost as if you too, at that moment, introduced you to yourself. When you turn the light on from the inside, you have a different glow about you that others may not recognize. Re-introduce yourself.

The ability to transform and remain aware of your progress is key to staying influential to your being. This is about having an expertise in keeping what you possess in your power, in your power - no matter what. The power is self-awareness, and what it allows for you to control is self. Sure, things happen beyond our control, but it doesn't mean we lose our sense of self. When things are outside of your control, you have to know yourself enough to make adjustments. If you got caught by surprise, know enough of what needs to be transformed in you to make it work and re-introduce yourself.

When we feel forced to accept something, we suffer. The most resistance will come from the unprepared. A transformation of self does not always have to come at a time when you need it most. You must stay in the habit of evolving and growing. This way you stay aware of who you were, who you are, and who you want to be. An awareness of self, whether you are preparing for change or not, is necessary to avoid unnecessary sufferance. Experiencing heartache can be damaging to your ego. If you fall short on loving self, others will too. Make a habit of re-introducing yourself to you.

People will try you and I know you know that, but it must be restated. Again, if you don't have to suffer, don't. Life already has its ups and downs, twists and turns. There are enough unknown variables to figure out for self to add more obscurity through the management of others. Once someone has introduced themselves to you as incompatible, or once they have demonstrated your interest is unmatched, before you have to curb your sufferance, re-introduce yourself.

Let's Practice!

Change is inevitable. Welcome change, it suits you best. When you have found yourself stuck to the same routine, and forced to make change – create a new you! Go ahead, even if you don't even know the new you, create someone you would love.

Who do you think you are?

Mastering others is a strength. Mastering yourself is true power. Lao Tzu

Step 10

Act Accordingly

I wish saying goodbye was as easy as reading steps 1, 2, and 3. Unfortunately, it is not. More importantly, though, heartache may not be a once-in-a-lifetime event. Oftentimes you can get your facts mixed up with your belief, which presents as hopes and wishes. Hope and wishing is the language of your heart, but can easily lead your heart into an unhealthy, inflated sense of self. Acting as though only your love keeps everything together will leave you exhausted and spent. If you haven't heard, in love, it takes two to tango. It is never just about the love you offer. Accept it and act accordingly.

Radical acceptance is not "getting over it." Acceptance, here, in this moment, is about recognition and actions of accordance. In the end, all we want is peace. All anyone will want is peace. You may not see that in the beginning, but all you want is to be free from your pain and heartache. In the universe, that could mean many things, though. You can be freed by someone returning their love for yours, and you can also be free by no longer allowing someone to be a source of contention for your desires. If someone does not want you, you cannot want them. As Ghandi once said, "Outward peace is useless without inner peace." Admit you were wrong about this person. Accept it and act accordingly.

I know. They were able to hide so much of who they truly were, or suddenly they have become someone you could no longer recognize. Either way, peace will only come from your acknowledgement of reality, and coming to terms personally with your loss. No one can offer you peace. Again, another thing that is in your possession and power. How do you define peace?

What can you think, feel, or do to get to this peaceful place? Because in the end, all you should be striving for is peace, whatever that is. Accept it and act accordingly.

Remember, anything which creates resistance is resistant to change. Change may not always be welcomed, but it is necessary. Once we become uncomfortable with our reality, we must change to become more familiar. It is how we ease our anxiety about things we may have been unaware of. Once more, a new you will want new things, and because of that, acceptance is key to acting accordingly. We cannot obtain peace holding grudges from past battles. Unpack your knapsack with acceptance and understand that some things do fall apart, but that doesn't mean you have to. Accept loss and act accordingly.

Let's Practice!

Peace can be defined in many ways. The most important thing to remember: is when peace is within you, nothing external to you can disturb it. Find your peace. Make it real enough so it may be called upon like a superpower when the external world is beyond your control.

Pathways to Peace
Thoughts that give me peace
Feelings that keep me at peace
Places that bring me peace

It's not the strongest of species that survives, not the most intelligent, but the one most responsive to change. – Charles Darwin

Means to an End

We need this; I needed this!

So, are you over it? If not, please refer to the beginning of the book and read through it again and as many times as you need to until it clicks! Relationships are hard, no matter who we are engaging with or the type of relationship we in engage in. It is my hope that this book can be a guide to keeping relationships healthy for all who are involved. Most importantly, for those who are reluctant to love for fear of heartache or past hurts. Unfortunately, all things can fall apart but it doesn't mean you have to. We don't wish for it (I don't want anyone to have the perspective that it cannot be avoided), but it is a part of some relationships we develop.

If ever you need to find your way back to self, this book is the tool, and a reference to self. I want it to be used as the marked trail back to you. I even come back to these steps over and over and every time I feel empowered to move forward. That is what I want it to do for whoever reads it. So, take a chance on love. See what's out there. And if you have to find your way back, use this book as the trail.

www.ingramcontent.com/pod-product-compliance
Lightning Source LLC
Chambersburg PA
CBHW031617040426
42452CB00006B/571